DATE DUE

OC 1 0 7		

DEMCO 38-296

PHYSICAL SCIENCE IN DEPTH

LIGHT

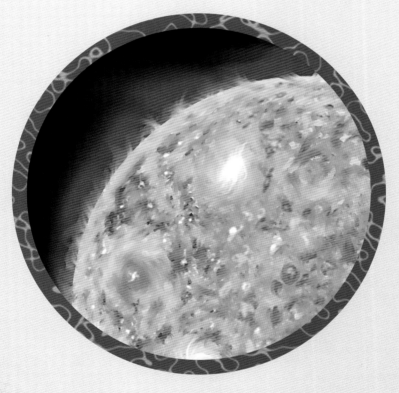

Alfred J. Smuskiewicz

Heinemann Library
Chicago, Illinois

Customer Service 888-454-2279
Visit our website at www.heinemannlibrary.com

Produced for Heinemann Library by White-Thomson Publishing Ltd.
Illustrations: Kerry Flaherty and Q2A Solutions
Photo Research: Amy Sparks
Production: Duncan Gilbert
Printed and bound in China by South China Printing Company Ltd.

12 11 10 09 08
10 9 8 7 6 5 4 3 2 1

Library of Congress Cataloging-in-Publication Data
Smuskiewicz, Alfred J.
  Light / Alfred J. Smuskiewicz.
      p. cm. — (Physical science in depth)
  Includes bibliographical references and index.
  ISBN 978-1-4034-9929-5 (library binding – hardcover)
  ISBN 978-1-4034-9937-0 (pbk.)
  1. Light—Juvenile literature. I. Title.
  QC360.S63 2008
  535—dc22

                                    2007006270

Acknowledgments
The author and publishers are grateful to the following for permission to reproduce copyrighted
material: Alamy **pp. 8** (Phototake Inc.), **47** (Travelshots.com); Corbis **pp. 13**, **42** (EPA),
48 (Walter Geiersperger); Istockphoto.com **title page** (George Argyropoulos), **pp. 5** (Joshua Haviv),
6 (George Argyropoulos), **10**, **11** (Brandon Laufenberg), **16** (Paul Reid), **18** (Frank Leung),
19 (Roman Krochuk), **23**, **26** (Nicholas Monu), **34** (Lief Cuyvers), **35** (Ekaterina Fribus),
45 (Brian Stanback); NASA **pp. 22** (ESA/J. Hester and A. Loll, Arizona State Univ.), **27**, **43**, **53**
(WMAP Science Team), **54** (ESA/S. Beckwith, STScI/the HUDF Team), **59**; Science Photo Library
pp. 9 (Klaus Guldbrandsen), **39** (Steve Gschmeissner), **52** (NASA/ESA/STScI/High-Z Supernova
Search Team), **57** (Fermilab); Topfoto **pp. 24** (Cornell University/Thomas Eisner), **44** (HIP);
United States Department of Defense **p. 25**.

Cover photograph of a prism separating white light into the colors of the visible spectrum is
reproduced with permission of Alamy/Phototake Inc.

Every effort has been made to contact copyright holders of any material reproduced in this book.
Any omissions will be rectified in subsequent printings if notice is given to the publisher.

The publishers would like to thank Ann Fullick, Timothy Griffin, and Barbara Bakowski for their
assistance in the preparation of this book.

Contents

Words printed in the text in bold, **like this**, are explained in the Glossary.

Surrounded by Light

Look around and you will notice that you are surrounded by light. Outside, the Sun shines its warm light all over Earth's surface. Inside, electric lamps light our homes. Our eyes perceive this light—this is how we see things.

Without the light from the Sun, life on Earth would not be possible. Because of light, we have food to eat. Plants use light from the Sun to power chemical reactions. These reactions make high-energy food in a process called **photosynthesis**. The plants use some of this energy to grow. People and other animals get some of the energy when they eat plants—or when they eat other animals that ate the plants. A by-product of photosynthesis is oxygen, which is released into the air. People and other animals draw this oxygen into their lungs to breathe.

VISIBLE LIGHT AND INVISIBLE LIGHT

The light we see—from the Sun or electric lights—makes up only a very small percentage of light in the universe. What we think of as light is the visible part of a band of energy called the **electromagnetic spectrum**. Ultraviolet light (such as the light in Sun lamps); infrared light (also known as heat); and X-rays (commonly used in medicine) are other types of electromagnetic energy. The electromagnetic spectrum also includes gamma rays, microwaves, and radio waves. Scientists often refer to all types of electromagnetic energy as "light."

USEFUL LIGHT

For thousands of years, people have watched the way that light behaves. Light seems to glisten on the surface of a pond—a phenomenon known as reflection. Light seems to change direction as it passes through water—this is refraction. Such observations

Electricity lights up our world, allowing cities such as New York (above) to thrive even at night.

have led to the application of light in many kinds of tools, including lenses, eyeglasses, microscopes, and telescopes.

Less than 150 years ago, the only light that people could use came from the Sun, fire, and simple inventions, such as candles and oil lamps. A new era dawned in the late 1800s, when people began to use electricity to create artificial light. Since then, people have gained a deeper understanding of light. They have used this understanding in many inventions, such as cameras, televisions, laser surgery, DVDs, and solar energy systems.

Today, research based on principles of light is even helping scientists answer such profound questions as how the universe began and what its ultimate fate will be.

The Nature of Light

The Sun is our most important source of light. The production of the Sun's light begins in its deepest layer, called the core. **Atoms** of hydrogen in the core combine in a type of reaction called **nuclear fusion**. Nuclear fusion is made possible by the extremely high pressures and temperatures inside the Sun's core. This combination releases energy in the form of light and heat.

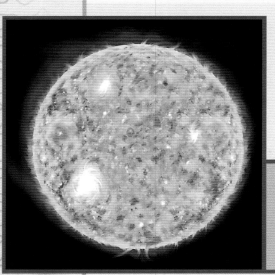

Light is a type of energy called **electromagnetic radiation** that can travel through space. Electromagnetic radiation flows through space like waves of water that ripple across the surface of a lake when you toss a rock into the water.

Nature's greatest sources of light are the billions of stars in the universe, including the Sun.

HOW WAVES ARE MEASURED

Imagine waves of water traveling across the surface of a lake or an ocean. The waves have a curved shape, with high spots and low spots occurring over and over. The waves have a number of other features, including **wavelength**, **frequency**, and **amplitude**. These are all different ways that waves can be measured.

Wavelength is the distance from the peak (high point) or trough (low point) of one wave to the peak or trough of the next.

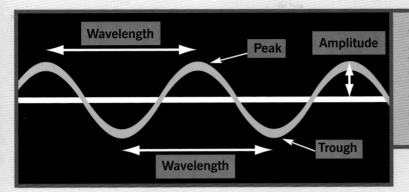

Wavelength and amplitude are two features that all types of electromagnetic radiation share, though these features can vary greatly from one type of wave to another.

Frequency is the number of waves that pass a particular point per second. Amplitude is the distance from a peak or trough to the midpoint of a wave.

The energy of a wave of light is related to its amplitude, frequency, and wavelength. The greater the amplitude or frequency, the higher the energy of the wave. The longer the wavelength, the lower the energy.

PARTICLE NATURE OF LIGHT

In addition to behaving like waves, electromagnetic radiation moves as pointlike particles—like billiard balls rolling across the surface of a pool table. German-born physicist Albert Einstein (1879–1955) revolutionized the world of physics in the early 1900s when he first developed the idea that light also exists as particles. These particles are called photons. Photons are produced by the nuclear fusion that takes place in the Sun.

Unlike other particles, photons have no **mass**. They are not made of matter, and they carry no weight. Photons are more like particles of energy that travel outward from a source, whether it is the Sun or a flashlight. These photons travel in ways that resemble the behavior of waves.

Did you know...?

Each photon emitted by the Sun takes about eight minutes to reach your eyes. Because of this, you see the Sun as it appeared eight minutes ago.

THE COLORS OF THE RAINBOW

Sunlight is made of the entire rainbow of colors, from violet (which has the shortest wavelength) to red (which has the longest wavelength). We normally see these colors mixed together, which makes each individual color impossible to see. As a result, the light we see appears as white light.

A **prism** allows us to see the different colors of light. A prism is a glass or **quartz** object with two parallel bases joined by three or more sides. It changes the direction of a beam of light by bending the light. The angle at which the light is bent depends on its wavelength. Thus, each wavelength of light appears as a different color. The spreading of white light into its various colors is called **dispersion**.

We can also see the colors of sunlight separated, or dispersed, in rainbows. That is because raindrops in the atmosphere bend light the same way that prisms do.

KEY EXPERIMENT Make Your Own Rainbow

You can make your own rainbow by projecting sunlight through a prism onto a piece of white paper. You can also separate white light into various colors by cutting a thin slit in black construction paper. Place the paper over the glass of an overhead projector in a darkened room. Hold a prism close to the projector, within the light beam made by the slit. The prism should project a color spectrum onto the wall.

A prism disperses white light into the various colors of the rainbow. Red light bends the least because it has the longest wavelength.

The mineral substances that coat the glow-in-the-dark hands on a watch give off light by luminescence. The brightness of the hands gradually weakens after the lights in the room are turned off. That is because the light energy absorbed by the hands is gradually used up.

OTHER SOURCES OF LIGHT

When the Sun gives off light, it also gives off heat. This type of light production—in which heat is emitted with light—is called **incandescence**. Some objects can give off light without emitting much, if any, heat. This type of light production is called **luminescence**.

Materials that naturally glow through luminescence are used to make devices that can be seen in the dark. If you've ever seen glow-in-the-dark hands on a watch or clock, you've seen luminescence. The hands are made of materials that give off light after they absorb light. These materials naturally give off light in a chemical process that does not give off heat.

People have invented various devices that produce light. Some of these inventions produce light through incandescence; others through luminescence.

Did you know...?

Luminous intensity, the amount of light produced by a source, used to be measured in units called candles. One of these units was equal to the amount of light given off by a medium-sized candle made from the oil of a sperm whale.

ELECTRIC LIGHTS

The most common lightbulbs are a type of incandescent light—they give off heat as well as light. If you've ever accidentally touched a lightbulb that has been switched on for a few minutes, you know that it can get hot enough to burn your finger. Thomas Edison (1847–1931) invented the first practical incandescent lightbulb in 1879. It is still the main type of electric light used today.

The part of a lightbulb that produces light is a thin, coiled wire called the filament. The wire is usually made of tungsten, a strong metal that can withstand vast amounts of heat without melting. An electric current flows through the filament, heating it to temperatures greater than 4,500°F (2,480°C). This extreme heat causes the filament to give off light.

Did you know...?

When an incandescent lightbulb burns out, tungsten from the filament evaporates and spreads over the inside surface of the bulb. That is the dark material you see inside a burnt-out bulb.

SCIENCE PIONEERS Thomas Edison: Lightbulbs

Though Thomas Edison is famous for inventing the incandescent lightbulb, several inventors before him had already developed incandescent lights. The problem with those lights, however, was that they needed batteries and quickly burned out. Edison invented an incandescent bulb with a long-lasting filament—and a system for lighting his bulbs by distributing electricity over wires from power stations to customers.

FLUORESCENT AND NEON LIGHTS

Fluorescent and neon lightbulbs are types of electric lights that produce luminescent light. The long white tubes you see in many ceiling lights are fluorescent lights. They produce light by passing an electric current through gas made of mercury and argon. The electric current causes the gas to give off ultraviolet light, which is invisible. (Ultraviolet light will be discussed in more detail in Chapter 4.) This ultraviolet energy, in turn, causes chemical substances called **phosphors** inside the tube to give off visible light but very little heat.

Many of the colorful lights you see on buildings at night in the shapes of words or pictures are neon lights. The color you see in a neon lightbulb depends on the gas used in the bulb. Some of these lights contain pure neon gas. Pure neon gas gives off a reddish-orange color when an electric current passes through it. If you add mercury gas to the neon in the bulb, it makes the light blue. Other gases produce other colors, depending on the wavelengths that make up their light.

A glowing neon sign is an effective tool for attracting customers to businesses that are open at night. Neon lights are a form of electric light known as gaseous-discharge lamps, which produce light by passing electric currents through gases.

Behavior of Light

You may not think of light *behavior* the same way you think of animal behavior. Yet light does behave in certain ways that you can observe. Light travels at a certain speed and moves through or bounces off different substances in different ways.

COSMIC SPEED LIMIT

Just as there is a speed limit on the highway, there is also a speed limit in the universe—the speed of light in a **vacuum**. A vacuum is an empty space with no air, such as exists in outer space. The speed at which photons travel in a vacuum is 186,282 miles (299,792 kilometers) per second. As far as scientists know, nothing in the universe can travel faster than this.

Scientists use the speed of light to measure the vast distances in the universe. The main unit of distance measurement in space is the **light-year**. A light-year is the distance that light travels in one year—5.88 trillion miles (9.46 trillion kilometers).

SCIENCE PIONEERS Lene Hau: Slowing the Speed of Light

In 1999, physicist Lene Hau (born 1959) of Harvard University in Cambridge, Massachusetts, lowered the speed of light to just 38 miles (61 kilometers) per hour. She and her team accomplished this feat by packing atoms of sodium together very tightly at extremely low temperatures and high pressures. When a light beam is passed through such densely packed matter, the particles of the substance get in the way of the photons. The light "takes on a more human dimension—you can almost touch it," says Hau.

The closest star to Earth (other than the Sun) is Proxima Centauri, which is just over four light-years away. That means it takes the light emitted by this star just over four years to reach Earth. Most of the stars we see in the sky are hundreds or thousands of light-years away.

When people talk about the speed of light, they are referring to the speed in a vacuum. Light does not move as quickly when it passes through other substances, such as air, water, or glass.

KEY EXPERIMENT Estimating the Speed of Light

In 1675, Danish astronomer Olaus Roemer (1644–1710) estimated the speed of light to within 25 percent of its actual speed using only a telescope! He did this by carefully observing how the moons of Jupiter disappeared behind the giant planet for lengths of time that varied with the changing distance between Jupiter and Earth. The farther Jupiter was from Earth, the longer the moons were blocked by Jupiter. That is because it took longer for the light from these objects to reach Earth.

The Andromeda Galaxy is so far away that the light we see coming from it took two million years to reach Earth. Because of this, scientists say that this galaxy is two million light-years away.

REFLECTION

Light is reflected when it strikes a surface and then rebounds off the surface either straight back or at an angle. The angle at which the light strikes the surface is called the **angle of incidence**. The angle at which the light rebounds is called its **angle of reflection**. The angle of reflection is always the same as the angle of incidence but in the opposite direction.

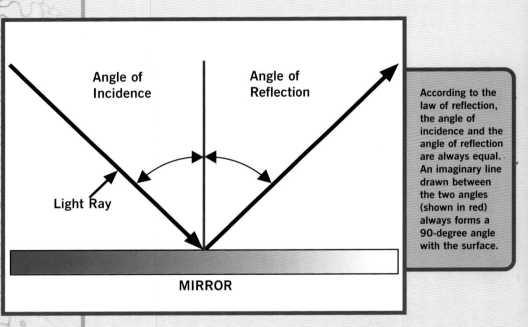

Angle of Incidence

Angle of Reflection

Light Ray

MIRROR

According to the law of reflection, the angle of incidence and the angle of reflection are always equal. An imaginary line drawn between the two angles (shown in red) always forms a 90-degree angle with the surface.

All the light rays that strike a smooth surface, such as a mirror, are reflected in the same direction. But when light strikes a rough surface, such as a gravel road, the light rays are reflected in many different directions. That is because light hits different parts of the rough surface at different angles of incidence, thereby producing different angles of reflection.

Light reflected off objects enters your eyes—this is how you see things. Different types of chemical compounds in objects reflect light of different wavelengths; these wavelengths determine the colors of objects. For example, the compounds in the skin of an apple reflect red wavelengths of light; a banana reflects yellow wavelengths.

TYPES OF MATERIALS

Transparent, or see-through, materials, such as regular window glass, let light waves pass straight through them. These materials reflect very little light to your eyes, which is why you can easily see through them. **Translucent** materials, such as frosted glass, let some light rays pass through them, but the rays are scattered in many different directions. Thus, you cannot see clearly through translucent materials. **Opaque** materials block all light, so you cannot see through them at all.

REFLECTING TELESCOPES

The principle of reflection is used in many devices, including reflecting telescopes. A reflecting telescope has a large mirror at one end of a tube. The mirror is **concave**, or curved inward. This bowl-shaped mirror reflects incoming light waves to a small, flat mirror inside the telescope tube. The flat mirror then directs the light waves to a point at which the user views the focused image through lenses in an eyepiece. A lens in the eyepiece magnifies the image, allowing the user to see a clear image of a distant object.

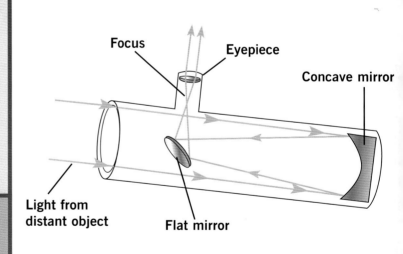

Focus

Eyepiece

Concave mirror

Light from distant object

Flat mirror

In a reflecting telescope, light rays are reflected from one mirror to another to create an image.

Did you know...?

Legendary British physicist Sir Isaac Newton (1642–1727) created the first practical reflecting telescope in 1668. However, the idea for a reflecting telescope was first described by the lesser-known Scottish astronomer James Gregory (1638–1675) five years earlier.

REFRACTION

Instead of reflecting light, many materials allow light to pass through them. When light passes through some materials, the light appears to bend. This bending is called refraction.

Refraction happens because different substances change the speed of light to different extents. For example, water slows light more than air does because the **molecules** of water are packed together more tightly than the molecules of air. As the speed of the light changes when it passes from water to air, the light is refracted.

You can see refraction by looking at a straw in a glass of water. The light from the part of the straw sticking out of the water passes through only the air to your eyes. But the light from the bottom part of the straw has to pass through the water and air. Because these light rays refract at the water's surface, the part of the straw that is in the water appears to be bent.

Refracted light can play tricks on your eyes. Because the speed of light is slower in water than in air, the light is refracted—and the straws appear to break.

REFRACTING TELESCOPES

Some telescopes are based on the principle of refraction. A refracting telescope has a large lens, called the objective, at the far end of a long tube. The lens is **convex**, or curved outward in the center. This lens refracts the light waves from a distant object so that all the waves meet at a point inside the tube. The user views the image through the eyepiece, which includes a second convex lens that magnifies the image.

Convex lens

Focus

Eyepiece

Light from distant object

A refracting telescope uses lenses instead of the mirrors used in reflecting telescopes. It uses convex lenses to magnify images in much the same way that a magnifying glass does.

CASE STUDY Mirages

Have you ever seen what appears to be a pool of water in the middle of a hot road—only to reach that spot to see that the pool has vanished? That "pool" was only an **optical illusion** called a mirage. Mirages are caused by the refraction of light. Rays of sunlight pass from the dense cool air high above the ground to the less dense warm air near the ground. The speed of the light increases as it enters the warm air, causing the light rays to bend. The bent rays appear as a wiggly image, like waves on the water, on the ground.

ABSORPTION

The colors of objects depend not only on the wavelengths of light that the objects reflect. The colors we see also depend on the wavelengths that the objects absorb.

As light hits an object, only some of the light is reflected. The rest of the light is absorbed. When you look at a fire engine, you see red. That is because the truck reflects the red wavelengths of light, while the rest of the light—such as the blue, green, and yellow wavelengths—is absorbed by the truck. You see only the reflected wavelengths. White objects reflect almost all the waves that strike them. Black objects absorb nearly all the waves that strike them.

Everything that we see reflects some colors of light and absorbs others. Which colors are reflected by the feathers of the cardinal in this picture? Which colors are absorbed?

DIFFRACTION

Diffraction of light happens when the waves of light pass through very small openings or near the edges of small objects. The openings or objects need to be about the same size as the light wavelengths. This causes the light waves to spread out, much like water from a hose spurts in all directions when you put your thumb over the opening. Diffraction can cause the edges of images seen through high-powered microscopes to be blurry as the light rays pass through the microscope.

SCATTERING

Some materials are made of very tiny particles that allow light to pass through, but when the light rays strike the particles, the rays are sent off in new directions. This process is called **scattering**.

Scattering causes the color of the sky. When light rays strike the gas molecules of nitrogen and oxygen in the air, the molecules cause the light to go off, or scatter, in different directions. On a clear day, most of the short blue wavelengths are scattered toward our eyes by the air molecules, causing us to see the sky as blue.

However, when the Sun is very low in the sky at sunset, its light rays enter the atmosphere at a lower angle. The rays then have to pass through more of the atmosphere than when the Sun is directly overhead. As a result, blue and other short wavelengths are scattered away before they reach our eyes. Only the longest wavelengths, the red ones, make it through the thick blanket of air to our eyes.

CASE STUDY Auroras

An **aurora** is a natural display of colored lights that can be seen in the night sky near Earth's poles. Auroras are caused by particles flowing from the Sun in a cosmic stream called the **solar wind**. Earth is surrounded by an invisible magnetic field. These electrically charged particles from the Sun become trapped near the north and south poles of Earth's magnetic field. When the particles collide with atoms in the atmosphere, energy is released. Some of this energy appears in the form of colored light.

Light in the Electromagnetic Spectrum

The light that we see makes up only a narrow zone of wavelengths within the electromagnetic spectrum. This zone is called the **visible spectrum**. All other kinds of electromagnetic radiation—gamma rays, X-rays, ultraviolet rays, infrared rays, microwaves, and radio waves—are made of wavelengths that are either longer or shorter than those of visible light. We cannot see these types of radiation with our eyes alone, though scientists have developed many technologies to detect, study, and use this radiation.

All forms of electromagnetic radiation have certain common characteristics. They all behave like both waves and particles, depending on the experiment used to observe them. The waves and particles of all electromagnetic radiation travel through space at the speed of light. All electromagnetic radiation can be reflected, refracted, and diffracted.

WAVELENGTHS AND FREQUENCIES

The main differences between one form of electromagnetic radiation and another are wavelength and frequency. Different wavelengths and frequencies result in different locations on the electromagnetic spectrum, different characteristics in nature, and different applications by people.

The longer the wavelength of any kind of electromagnetic radiation, the lower the energy level of the radiation. The higher the frequency, the greater the energy. Gamma rays have the shortest wavelength and the greatest frequency and produce the most energy. Radio waves have the longest wavelength, the lowest frequency, and the lowest energy. Visible light has wavelengths in the middle of the electromagnetic spectrum.

Did you know...?

Sir Isaac Newton published his many important discoveries about light in his book *Opticks* in 1704. Newton's discoveries led to the modern understanding of the electromagnetic spectrum. Newton used the word *spectrum* to describe the way light appears as many different colors. *Spectrum* means "appearance" in Latin.

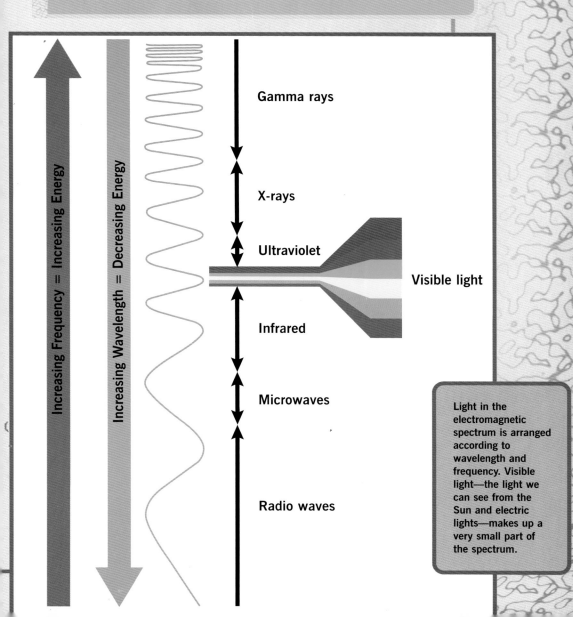

Increasing Frequency = Increasing Energy

Increasing Wavelength = Decreasing Energy

Gamma rays

X-rays

Ultraviolet

Visible light

Infrared

Microwaves

Radio waves

Light in the electromagnetic spectrum is arranged according to wavelength and frequency. Visible light—the light we can see from the Sun and electric lights—makes up a very small part of the spectrum.

GAMMA RAYS

Gamma rays have the highest energy of all forms of electromagnetic radiation. They are given off by radioactive materials, such as uranium, which is used to produce energy in nuclear power plants. Very small amounts of gamma rays constantly enter our bodies from naturally radioactive material in the air and soil. Because we are exposed to very low levels, these rays are normally harmless to people. However, if enough of these rays go into a body over time, they can cause changes in the body's cells that might lead to cancer and other diseases.

Despite their potential for harm, gamma rays can be useful to us. In hospitals, high doses of gamma rays that are directed at cancer cells can destroy them. Gamma rays are also used to destroy bacteria in food—a process called **irradiation**—and on surgical instruments. In addition, gamma rays can be used with special cameras to make images of chemical activity inside the brain—this image is called a positron emission tomography (PET) scan.

Gamma rays are also useful in giving scientists information about the universe. Astronomers detect gamma rays emitted by various cosmic sources, including exploding stars called **supernovae** and clouds of gas and dust called **nebulae**. Analysis of these rays provides information about the sources. Astronomers learn, for example, how much energy is released when a star explodes.

Astronomers have found that the highest-energy gamma rays ever detected come from the Crab Nebula. The Crab Nebula is a giant cloud of gas and dust that formed when a star exploded. This amazing event was visible from Earth more than 900 years ago.

X-RAYS

If you have ever had a broken bone or been to the dentist for a checkup, you are probably familiar with X-rays. Doctors and dentists take X-ray pictures of parts of your body. These photos, called radiographs, allow medical professionals to diagnose and treat medical problems.

X-rays can pass through your body tissues but are absorbed by your bones or teeth. The rays that pass through your body are detected on sheets of special film or plastic to make photographs of your bones, teeth, or internal organs. On the resulting image, soft tissues show up as dark areas and your bones and teeth show up as white.

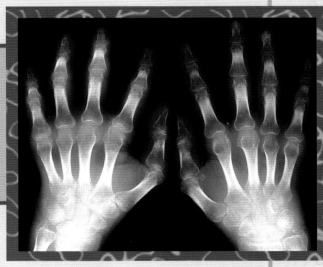

An X-ray image clearly shows the finger and wrist bones of two hands. Bones and other hard tissue absorb more of the rays than the muscles and other soft tissue do, so the bones show up much more clearly on a special film or plastic.

Too many X-rays can be harmful. Doctors often cover parts of a patient's body with a lead apron, which blocks the X-rays, so the rays enter only the part of the body being examined.

X-rays have other uses, too. Some manufacturers use X-rays to check for flaws inside aluminum and steel items and computer chips. Some telescopes can detect X-rays emitted by certain cosmic objects, such as objects falling into **black holes**. Black holes are regions of space with such powerful **gravity** that nothing can escape from them. Detecting these X-rays is one of the few ways that scientists can find black holes.

ULTRAVIOLET RAYS

Ultraviolet (UV) radiation is electromagnetic radiation with wavelengths that are *just* too short to be visible. The invisible ultraviolet rays that reach Earth's surface from the Sun are a powerful form of energy.

Some exposure to ultraviolet rays is good for you. Ultraviolet rays help your body produce vitamin D, which is needed for bone strength. Doctors even treat some patients with moderate doses of UV rays to help treat skin conditions, such as acne and psoriasis. High doses of UV rays can also be helpful in destroying bacteria on surgical instruments. However, if you are exposed to too much ultraviolet radiation, you might end up with a painful sunburn or even skin cancer.

A flower, as seen by human eyes (right), reflects only ordinary light in visible wavelengths. But that same flower, as seen by the eyes of a bee (left), gives off wavelengths of ultraviolet light. Dark markings on the flower seen in ultraviolet light help guide insects to the flower's nectar and pollen.

RECENT DEVELOPMENTS Far Ultraviolet Spectroscopic Explorer

The Far Ultraviolet Spectroscopic Explorer (FUSE) is a satellite that observes cosmic objects in ultraviolet light. FUSE **orbits** 500 miles (800 kilometers) above Earth's surface. FUSE has made many important discoveries, including finding large regions of hot gas surrounding our Milky Way galaxy and other galaxies. This gas gives off ultraviolet light that can be detected by FUSE.

INFRARED RAYS

Infrared radiation is electromagnetic radiation with wavelengths that are *just* too long to be visible. Infrared rays are the same thing as heat—they cause you to feel warmth. You feel the warmth of the Sun and heat from a fireplace because of the infrared rays that are given off by the Sun and fire.

All warm objects—even your own body—give off infrared radiation. The warmer an object, the more infrared radiation it gives off. Special cameras, binoculars, and telescopes allow people to see infrared radiation. These devices help police, firefighters, and military personnel find people in the dark or in smoky places.

You use infrared rays every time you click a button on a remote control. An electronic chip inside your TV remote control senses when you press a button on the remote to change the channel. A small lightbulb called a light-emitting diode (LED) then shoots a ray of infrared light out from the remote to a receiver in your TV, which causes the channel to change.

The use of special binoculars allows this U.S. Air Force plane to be clearly seen in the dark of night. Such night-vision binoculars work by collecting tiny amounts of visible light and combining it with the infrared light (heat) emitted by objects. An electronic device in the binoculars then multiplies the number of photons collected, allowing the objects to be easily seen. Night-vision images are shown in green because the human eye can detect more shades of green than any other color.

MICROWAVES

Most people think of microwaves as kitchen appliances that cook food quickly. Microwaves are actually a type of radio wave. Their wavelengths are much longer than those of other types of radiation, but they are shorter than those of other radio waves. Like all radio waves, microwaves can easily pass through rain, smoke, gas, dust, and other material without interference. These properties make microwaves useful in radar systems and for long-distance communication, such as in some cell phones and wireless computer networks. Scientists use microwaves to communicate with distant satellites and other spacecraft.

Microwaves make it possible for us to communicate over wireless networks. This allows us to check e-mail and use the Internet from almost anywhere.

RECENT DEVELOPMENTS Invisibility Cloak

Researchers at Duke University in North Carolina announced in October 2006 that they had invented an "invisibility cloak" for microwaves. The cloak is like a shield that can hide objects by bending microwaves. The cloak is made of special metals that are laid down in certain patterns. When a beam of microwaves reaches the cloak, the metal patterns cause the microwaves to bend around the object instead of being reflected back. If this cloaking device could be made to work with visible light waves—instead of just microwaves—it would make things disappear right before your eyes!

RADIO WAVES

It may seem odd to think that the type of energy that carries broadcast sound signals to your radio is related to light waves. However, both radio waves and light waves make up bands of frequencies in the electromagnetic spectrum. Radio waves have the longest wavelength—and the lowest energy—of all forms of electromagnetic radiation.

Radios are not the only appliances that pick up broadcast signals with radio waves. Televisions do, too. Navigators on airplanes and ships use radio waves to help them stay on course. Scientists use radio waves to communicate with spacecraft, such as *Voyager 1*, which is the most distant manmade object in the universe.

SCIENCE PIONEERS Heinrich Hertz: Measuring Waves

In the late 1800s, Heinrich Hertz (1857–94) showed that the back-and-forth movement, or **oscillation**, of electric charges could produce electromagnetic waves. Physicists later honored Hertz by adopting the *hertz* as the unit to measure frequencies of electromagnetic waves. The speed of FM (frequency modulation) radio waves ranges from 88 to 108 megahertz (million hertz), which is why the FM dial on your radio goes from 88 to 108. AM (amplitude modulation) radio waves range from 550 to 1,600 kilohertz (thousand hertz), which is why the AM dial on your radio goes from 550 to 1600.

Radio waves allow scientists to communicate with the *Voyager 1* spacecraft, which is on the very edge of the solar system, 9 billion miles (14 billion kilometers) from the Sun.

The Physics of Vision

Of the five senses, humans and many other animals rely most on vision. The importance we place on vision might be summarized best in the common phrase, "Seeing is believing!"

Our eyes are highly complex organs that work like natural cameras to take in light and make pictures. Special cells in our eyes convert the light into electrical signals, which our brain then translates into the images we see.

LETTING IN THE LIGHT

The process of vision begins when the rays of light reflected by objects enter your eye. Different-colored objects give off different wavelengths of light. The rays enter your eye through a small opening at the front of the eyeball called the pupil. The pupil is a hole in the iris, the ring of muscle that gives the eye its color. The iris controls the amount of light that enters your eye by changing the size of the pupil.

You can easily observe the changes in your pupil size in response to light by going into a dimly lit room and standing in front of a mirror. Shine a flashlight near your eyes (but not directly in them!). You will see your pupils shrink in size when the flashlight is on. When you turn the flashlight off, your pupils will increase in size again.

Did you know...?

The human eyeball is about 1 inch (25 millimeters) wide, approximately the size of a ping-pong ball. Each eyeball weighs about 1 ounce (28 grams)—roughly half the weight of a tennis ball.

BRINGING THINGS INTO FOCUS

The pupil is covered by the cornea, which is the clear outer part of the eyeball. The cornea refracts, or bends, light rays as they enter the eye to help bring all the rays together so that they are in focus.

After light rays pass through the pupil, they enter the lens. The lens of each eye refracts the light rays even more, so the rays come together at a point at the back of the eye. This point is where the light rays are in sharp focus.

For the lens to focus light rays properly, it must change shape as you look at different things. That is because light rays from objects enter the eyes at different angles, depending on how far away the objects are.

When you look at a house across the street, the light rays from the house are parallel as they enter your eye. To bring these rays into focus, the lens in your eye becomes flat and thin. But when you read a book, the light from the book spreads out as it enters your eye. To bring these light rays into focus, the lens becomes round and thick.

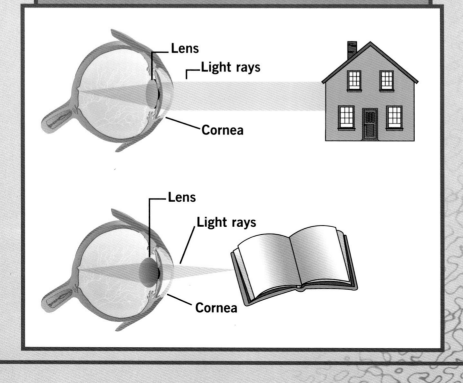

Lens

Light rays

Cornea

Lens

Light rays

Cornea

FROM LIGHT TO ELECTRICAL SIGNALS

After the light rays pass through the lens, the focused beam strikes the **retina**. The retina is the thin layer of cells at the inside back of the eyeball.

There are two main types of retina cells—rods and cones, the names of which describe their shapes. Both rods and cones absorb light and convert it into electrical signals. In each eye, we have more than 100 million rods and about six million cones. Rods are sensitive to shades of gray. Cones are sensitive to more than 200 colors. Rods function best in dim light; cones work best in bright light.

PERIPHERAL VISION

When you look directly at an object, its light rays are focused on a spot near the center of the retina. This cone-rich spot, called the **macula**, gives you the sharpest vision. Surrounding the macula is an area that is rod-rich. This area gives you your peripheral (side) vision—the things you notice off to the sides when you are focused on something else. Because rods work best in dim light, you can see peripheral objects more clearly at night.

RECENT DEVELOPMENTS New Type of Eye Cell Discovered

In 2002, neuroscientist (nerve scientist) David Berson (born 1954) and his colleagues at Brown University in Providence, Rhode Island, discovered a new type of light-sensitive cell in the eye's retina. Berson named these cells intrinsically photosensitive retinal ganglion cells (ipRGCs). Berson found that ipRGCs send signals to the brain about how light or dark it is outside. These signals control the body's **circadian rhythm**, the daily cycle of changes in a person's alertness, body temperature, and organ function. Your circadian rhythm is responsible for making you feel tired at night and awake during the day.

Did you know...?

The lens of the eye, like the lens of a camera, reverses images. Because of this, the images on the retina are upside down and flipped left to right. The brain instantaneously interprets this flipped image from the retina as right side up, enabling us to see properly.

FROM ELECTRICAL SIGNALS TO IMAGES

The electrical signals produced by rods and cones travel through nerve fibers in the retina to the optic nerve. The optic nerve is a cable of about one million nerve fibers that connects the retina to the brain.

Look up from this book, and think of all the visual information there is in your field of view, such as different colors, shapes, and levels of brightness. All of this information travels through the optic nerve to your brain. The brain puts all the details together and interprets the information as it really is.

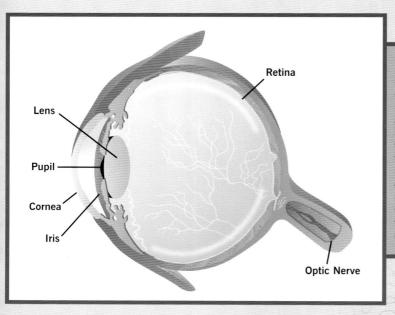

Retina

Lens

Pupil

Cornea

Iris

Optic Nerve

Light rays from objects are refracted by the clear cornea of the eye and pass through the pupil. After the rays are further refracted by the lens, they travel to the back of the eyeball, where an image of the objects comes into focus on the retina. Electrical signals representing the image travel through the optic nerve to the brain.

VISION PROBLEMS

A number of problems can develop with the eye's lens and other parts of vision. The two most common problems that can be corrected are **myopia**, or nearsightedness, and **hyperopia**, or farsightedness.

Nearsighted, or myopic, people have trouble seeing objects at a distance. Their lenses bring light rays from distant objects to a focus before they reach the retina. Farsightedness happens when the lens does not thicken enough to bring the light rays from nearby objects to a focus. Both problems can be corrected with eyeglasses, contact lenses, or surgery.

Eyeglasses are based on the way lenses work. A lens bends the light rays that pass through it. This bending causes the light rays to converge, or become narrower, on the other side of the lens. The light rays all come together at the focal point, where the image produced by the light waves is in focus.

Glasses or contact lenses to correct myopia are made from concave lenses, which push back the focal point to the retina. Glasses or contact lenses to correct hyperopia are made from convex lenses, which draw forward the focal point to the retina.

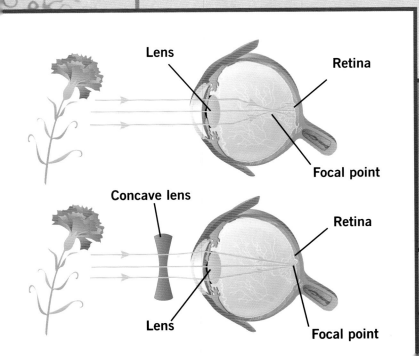

Lens

Retina

Focal point

Concave lens

Retina

Lens

Focal point

In myopia, or nearsightedness, light rays from far objects come into focus inside the eye before they reach the retina. Because of this, the image is out of focus. Glasses to correct myopia are made with lenses that stretch out the light rays so that they come into focus on the retina. This results in an image that is in focus.

Some people choose to correct myopia or hyperopia with laser surgery. In this procedure, surgeons reshape the cornea with a laser to refocus light rays onto the retina.

A cataract is a clouding of the eye's lens. It can cause partial or total loss of vision. Surgeons can replace the clouded lens with a clear plastic lens.

If someone is color blind, he or she has trouble telling certain colors from others. Color blindness is caused by chemical abnormalities in the cones. It is typically present at birth and cannot be corrected.

KEY EXPERIMENT Seeing Like Superman

Scientist and inventor William H. Dobelle (1941–2004) implanted the first vision-improving **electrodes** into blind patients' brains in the 1990s. The patients wore glasses that included a tiny video camera that captured the scene. A computer processor translated the image into a series of signals that were sent to the brain via the electrodes. This allowed the patients to see fuzzy images. Researchers believe that advanced brain implants might someday allow people to have better-than-normal vision—perhaps to even see infrared and ultraviolet light.

BLINDNESS

Some people are born blind because of problems with the visual center of the brain or the nerves that connect the eyes to the brain. Most of these cases cannot be corrected. Other people become blind later in life.

One of the common causes of blindness in adults is **diabetic retinopathy**. This condition can happen in people with diabetes, an illness in which the body cannot use a sugar called glucose. In diabetic retinopathy, blood vessels in the retina leak, close up, or grow too much, causing blood to fill the inside of the eyeball. Diabetic retinopathy can be corrected with surgery.

VISION IN OTHER ANIMALS

Many animals' eyes work very differently than human eyes do. The eyes of flatworms, for example, are just tiny light-sensitive spots. These eyespots tell the animal whether it is dark or light outside and in which direction to move to go toward the light. Such eyespots cannot form clear images of objects.

Many insects (such as flies and bees) and crustaceans (such as lobsters) have large compound eyes. Each compound eye is made of many tiny lenses. Each lens forms a small part of the total scene, and the animal's brain puts all the parts together to form a single image.

SQUIDS AND OCTOPUSES

The most advanced eyes among invertebrates, or animals without backbones, belong to squids and octopuses. The eyes of these sea creatures have highly sensitive retinas. Cells in the retinas can make out clear shapes and different light levels in the dark, murky depths of the ocean.

In human eyes, the lens is fixed in place but can change shape to focus on near or distant objects. The lenses in an octopus's eyes, however, actually move back and forth to give a sharp focus.

BIRDS AND MAMMALS

Some birds have the best vision in the animal world. Eagles and vultures, for example, can see small rodents and other details on the ground while flying at heights of more than 2 miles (3 kilometers). Their large eyes are packed with about four to five times the number of rods and cones that human eyes have, and their lenses can change focus very quickly.

Many mammals' eyes are specialized for night vision. A cat's eyes seem to glow in the dark because of a mirrorlike structure at the back of each eye. This structure reflects extra light onto the cat's retina, helping the animal see at night.

BIOLUMINESCENCE

Some animals, plants, fungi, and bacteria can produce their own light through a process called **bioluminescence**. In this process, atoms of chemicals in light-producing structures become excited. When the atoms return to their normal state, they give off energy as photons. Animals that use bioluminescence include lanternfish, jellyfish, and squids.

RECENT DEVELOPMENTS Robot Eyes

Researchers at the University of Buffalo in New York are trying to make electronic versions of the eyes of animals with the keenest vision, such as octopuses and eagles. Using technology similar to that in digital cameras, scientists hope to make improved vision systems for robots. Such robots might explore the deep sea, distant planets, and other places too dangerous for humans.

HOW PLANTS USE LIGHT

Of course plants cannot see, but they still need light to provide energy to live. Plants use photosynthesis to get energy from light. In this process, the energy from sunlight converts carbon dioxide and water into the chemical energy of food.

The conversion of light energy into chemical energy takes place in chloroplasts, which are tiny green structures in a plant's leaves. The energy of the light rays causes molecules of water to split into hydrogen and oxygen atoms. The hydrogen combines with carbon dioxide from the air to form a simple sugar. The plant uses this sugar to make carbohydrates, proteins, fats, and other food substances needed for growth.

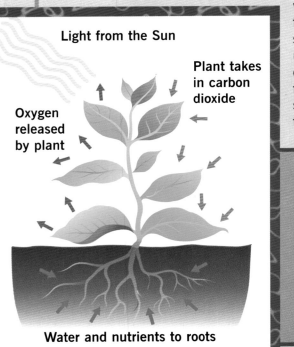

Light from the Sun

Plant takes in carbon dioxide

Oxygen released by plant

Water and nutrients to roots

Plants use the energy of sunlight to power the process of photosynthesis, in which carbon dioxide and water are combined to make carbohydrates (the plants' food). During photosynthesis, plants release oxygen into the atmosphere. People and other animals use this oxygen to breathe.

Did you know...?

The only place on Earth where organisms do not depend on light and photosynthesis for survival is at hydrothermal vents in the deepest, darkest areas of the ocean floor. There, bacteria use chemicals from the hydrothermal vents to produce energy to live.

RECENT DEVELOPMENTS Artificial Photosynthesis

Scientists at Brookhaven National Laboratory in New York City are trying to duplicate photosynthesis in the laboratory. Their goal is to create a type of artificial photosynthesis in which solar energy converts carbon dioxide into methanol and other organic (carbon-based) compounds. Such compounds could serve as inexpensive fuels and raw materials for the chemical industry.

ALBEDO EFFECT

Another way that light is important in nature is related to a phenomenon called the **albedo effect**, which plays a major role in controlling temperature and other aspects of Earth's climate.

Albedo is a measure of an object's brightness. An object that is perfectly white has an albedo of 1, meaning that it reflects all the light reaching it. A perfectly black object has an albedo of 0, meaning that it absorbs all the light reaching it. The albedo can be found by comparing the amount of light reflected by an object with the amount of light absorbed by that object.

The albedo of Earth's surface is always changing. When it snows, the snow reflects sunlight away from the surface, so the surface has a high albedo. When snow starts to melt, the surface begins to absorb more sunlight. This warms the surface, causing even more snow to melt. Then the surface absorbs more light than it reflects, and the surface has a lower albedo.

ROLE IN GLOBAL WARMING

People can have an effect on the albedo of the Earth. As people cut down forests, remove natural vegetation, and build cities, they change the albedo of those areas. Many streets, buildings, and other structures built by people absorb a great amount of sunlight, lowering the albedo.

This is important for global warming. Because buildings and streets absorb so much sunlight, cities become warmer than they would be if they had a natural cover of vegetation. This is one reason that temperatures around the world are increasing.

Special Uses for Light

People use light in many ways. The invention of devices based on principles of light has led to amazing advancements in medicine, astronomy, communications, entertainment, and energy production.

LIGHT IN MEDICINE

Medical researchers, physicians, and laboratory technicians all rely on technologies that use light in one way or another. Among the many applications of light in medicine are microscopes, endoscopic surgery, and laser surgery.

MICROSCOPES

Modern medical research and various lab tests would not be possible without microscopes. Microscopes use lenses to magnify cells, tissues, and other materials. The first true microscope was used in the 1670s by Anton van Leeuwenhoek (1632–1723) of the Netherlands. His single-lens microscope could magnify an object more than 250 times.

Many improvements in optical, or light, microscopes have been made since the time of Leeuwenhoek. Today, microscopes are essential tools in medical and scientific research, as well as in the diagnosis and treatment of disease. The most powerful optical microscopes today are called compound microscopes, which have two or more sets of lenses. Compound microscopes can magnify objects up to 2,000 times.

Magnification power is only one useful property of a microscope. A good microscope also has a high resolution—that means it can produce a sharp, clear image. Resolution tends to decrease as magnification power increases. This is because the more powerful lenses refract light so much that the bent rays may not come into focus.

The most advanced microscopes today, called electron microscopes, do not use lenses and light to magnify objects. They use beams of **electrons** and electric currents. Compared with a regular light microscope, an electron microscope can make a clearer picture of very small features because the waves of an electron beam are much closer together than the waves of visible light. An electron microscope can magnify a specimen so much that even some individual atoms can be seen.

Electron microscopes can give a very detailed look at objects—such as the human eyebrow hairs magnified 100 times here—by using beams of electrons and electric currents.

ENDOSCOPIC SURGERY

Many patients in hospitals are spared major surgery thanks to a procedure called endoscopic surgery. In this procedure, a surgeon inserts a tubelike instrument called an **endoscope** through a small cut in a patient's body. Endoscopes are made of bunches of thin fibers that transmit light. The light carries images from the inside of the body to a screen outside the body.

Endoscopic images enable surgeons to diagnose and treat diseases and injuries without making large cuts in patients' bodies. Patients undergoing endoscopic surgery recover much more quickly than those having traditional surgery.

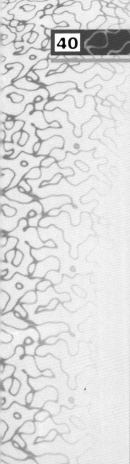

LASER SURGERY

You've probably seen lasers used as weapons in science fiction stories. In the real world, however, lasers are used in many industries and professions, including medicine.

A laser produces a narrow but powerful beam of light that can travel for vast distances without spreading out. In a typical laser, energy from electric power is supplied to a gaslike substance called plasma. Atoms in the plasma absorb the electrical energy and become excited. The atoms then release the extra energy as photons—light.

LASER LIGHT VS. ORDINARY LIGHT

Laser light differs from ordinary light in a few key ways. As we know, ordinary light is made up of all the colors of the visible spectrum. Laser light produces light of only one color. Also, a beam of laser light can travel without spreading out. And the light waves in a laser beam move in phase—with all the wave peaks together. This type of light is said to be **coherent**. In ordinary light, the light spreads out, and the peaks and troughs move out of phase. This type of light is **incoherent**.

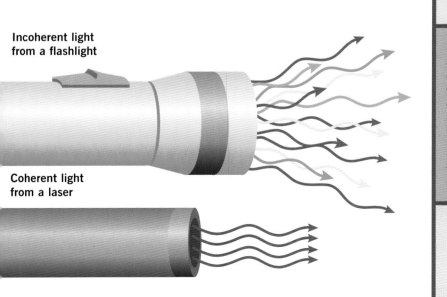

Incoherent light from a flashlight

Coherent light from a laser

The light from a flashlight includes all the wavelengths of the visible spectrum, each moving in random fashion. A laser beam, however, has light of only one wavelength, with all the peaks and troughs moving together.

SCIENCE PIONEERS Theodore Maiman: First Functioning Laser

In 1960, American physicist Theodore H. Maiman (born 1927) invented the first functioning laser at Hughes Research Laboratories in Malibu, California. The key idea behind lasers is a process called **stimulated emission**. This happens when a photon stimulates an atom to emit another photon. The second photon is of equal energy to, and moving in the same direction as, the first photon. Albert Einstein first described this idea in 1917, but it took many years before scientists could figure out how to apply it.

Surgeons use lasers for very precise cutting and sealing of blood vessels. LASIK surgery is a type of laser surgery that improves eyesight by correcting myopia and hyperopia. Surgeons reshape patients' corneas to refocus light rays onto the retinas. LASIK has become very popular over the past decade. In 2005 alone, about 1.3 million Americans had LASIK surgery.

LASIK surgery for both eyes usually takes 10 to 15 minutes to complete. Each pulse of the laser used in LASIK surgery removes approximately one-quarter of a micron of tissue from the patient's cornea—about 1/200th the thickness of a human hair—in about 12 billionths of a second.

There are also many types of cosmetic laser surgery. These include treatments to remove scars, wrinkles, body hair, excess fat, and tattoos.

Did you know...?

Distance can be measured with great accuracy by timing how long it takes a laser beam—traveling at the speed of light—to reach an object and reflect back from the object. Lasers have enabled scientists to measure the distance between Earth and the Moon to an accuracy within 2 inches (5 centimeters).

ASTRONOMY

Astronomers use telescopes to study objects that are so far away that they cannot be seen with the naked eye. Among the first researchers to conduct serious studies with telescopes were the Italian scientist Galileo (1564–1642) and the British scientist Sir Isaac Newton.

The two main kinds of optical (light) telescopes—refracting and reflecting telescopes—were discussed earlier. Some of these telescopes are very large. The larger and smoother the mirrors in a reflecting telescope, the higher the quality of the image.

Many other kinds of telescopes are used to study various forms of electromagnetic radiation, including radio waves, ultraviolet rays, and infrared rays. Some telescopes, such as the Hubble Space Telescope, orbit Earth.

This man is sitting in the center of the largest mirror used in an optical telescope. The mirror measures 27.5 feet (8.4 meters) in diameter. It was later finely polished and mounted alongside an identical mirror on the Large Binocular Telescope at the Mount Graham International Observatory in Arizona.

Because the Hubble Space Telescope orbits high above the atmosphere, which interferes with ground-based telescopes, it can make images of cosmic objects that are much sharper than the images produced by telescopes on Earth.

SPECTROMETERS

Astronomers—as well as chemists and other scientists—often analyze the chemical composition of objects with a device called a **spectrometer**. A spectrometer has a prism that spreads out light from an object into its spectrum of colors. Each type of chemical gives off light with a different pattern of colors, so scientists can tell which chemicals are in the object by the types of patterns made by the spectrometer. Astronomers use spectrometers with telescopes to analyze the chemical makeup of stars and planets.

RECENT DEVELOPMENTS Alien Atmospheres

In 2001, for the first time ever, astronomers used a spectrometer on the Hubble Space Telescope to study the atmosphere of a planet orbiting a star other than the Sun. The scientists determined that the atmosphere of a large planet 150 light-years away contains the element sodium. They also found that the atmosphere might contain methane, water vapor, potassium, and other chemicals. Astronomers believe that spectrometers on more powerful telescopes will enable them to study many other planets in the future.

CAMERAS

There are many different types of cameras today. Some use film to record images, and others record images digitally onto electronic cards. Some cameras take still pictures, and others make motion pictures. But all of these cameras have certain things in common—they work somewhat like artificial eyes.

Light enters the front of the camera through a lens. The lens focuses the light on a piece of film or on an electronic sensor at the back of the camera. The light causes chemical changes in film and electronic changes in sensors. These changes produce images of the scenes we see through the camera.

A good way to learn about light is to take pictures with a camera. Photographers can change the way light enters a camera to create different kinds of images. One way to do this is to use different types of lenses. Another way is to change the exposure—the amount of light that reaches the film or sensor. An overexposure results from too much light entering the camera, and an underexposure results from too little.

CASE STUDY The Camera Obscura

The first camera, called the camera obscura, was invented in Italy in about 1500. It was basically a large box with a small lens in one side that let light in. The light formed an upside-down image at the opposite end of the box. Later overhead versions (such as the one shown here) included a mirror that flipped the image right side up. The camera obscura was popular with artists, who traced the camera's images to help them paint accurate scenes. But the camera obscura could not make permanent pictures.

CDS AND DVDS

CDs and DVDs would not exist without lasers. As the discs are manufactured, the laser beam makes millions of tiny pits in the discs, which represent sounds or pictures. When you put a disc in your CD or DVD player, a different laser beam reads the pits. The laser light is reflected off the pits and translated by the player back into sounds and pictures.

FIBER-OPTIC COMMUNICATION

Fiber optics is a field that deals with transmitting light through transparent fibers of glass or plastic, called optical fibers. An optical fiber can be thinner than a hair, but these fibers can carry enormous amounts of information for hundreds of miles.

Fiber-optic communication systems begin with lasers that produce information consisting of rapidly flashing light. The flashes may represent pictures, sounds, or both. Instruments at the end of the fibers translate these flashes back into pictures and sounds.

A cable made of optical fibers can transmit much more information than a regular copper cable. This makes optical fibers very useful for communication systems. Many telephone companies and other communication companies use networks of fiber-optic cables across continents and under the sea.

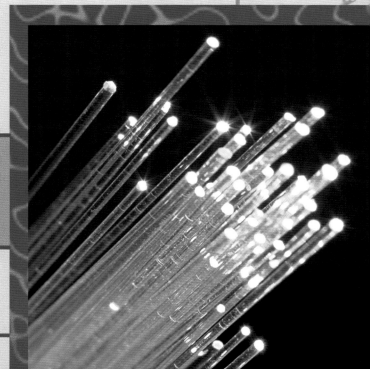

Cables made of optical fibers can transmit vast amounts of information in the form of flashing light for hundreds of miles—without any loss in the light's intensity.

MOVIE PROJECTORS

Some very familiar applications of light come from various forms of entertainment, including movies. A typical motion picture projector works by shining light from a bulb through a strip of film containing images. The light travels to a mirror inside the projector, the mirror reflects the light to a lens, and the lens projects the images onto the movie screen.

The way in which we view movies provides an interesting illustration of how the human eye perceives light and motion. A film is made up of a series of still images, called frames. These frames are projected so quickly, one after another, that instead of seeing a series of still images, our eyes see a moving image. Film is typically projected at 24 frames per second, so a two-hour movie includes 172,800 frames.

LASER LIGHT SHOWS

Laser light shows are spectacular displays of changing patterns of colorful light. These light displays are often set to dramatic music and are designed to thrill a crowd.

People who stage laser light shows use special computer software that can arrange the laser beams in moving and ever-changing patterns. The patterns can be made to resemble different objects. For example, a laser light show on the Fourth of July might include a giant waving American flag that changes into a soaring bald eagle.

Did you know...?

The film in an IMAX projection system has frames that are 10 times larger than those in a typical projector system. The film runs through an IMAX projector at 334 feet (102 meters) per minute—compared with 90 feet (27 meters) per minute for a typical projector. That means that a typical IMAX movie is made up of about 2 miles (3 kilometers) of film.

This laser light show was produced to entertain the crowd at the opening of the Tate Modern art gallery in London.

HOLOGRAPHY

Holography is a complex process involving the use of lasers to make three-dimensional (3-D) images called holograms. First, a laser beam is reflected off an object and onto a photographic plate. Then, other laser beams shine on the plate to make a particular pattern of light rays. The rays seem to come from above the plate, resulting in a 3-D image of the original object that seems to hover in space.

Holograms are used in various applications, such as making artwork, jewelry, and advertising displays. Most of the holograms we see today are simple light-reflecting displays on money, credit cards, and drivers' licenses that help prevent the counterfeiting of these items. Scientists hope to eventually make holograms that look more like real 3-D objects—and even like real people!

SOLAR ENERGY

One of the most exciting applications of light is solar energy, the use of energy from the Sun to produce electricity. Solar energy has the potential to provide us with an unlimited supply of energy that does not cause pollution or contribute to global warming. Thus, solar energy has important advantages over such fossil fuels as coal and petroleum, which are partially responsible for these environmental problems.

Unfortunately, the current solar energy technology is a very inefficient and expensive way to convert the Sun's energy into electrical power. That is mainly because sunlight is so thinly spread over such large areas that solar technology has trouble collecting and concentrating enough sunlight to produce usable power. As a result, solar power is responsible for less than one percent of the total energy consumption in the United States.

Some homes use solar energy to generate heat or electricity, and some industries use limited amounts of solar energy. However, solar power might become more important for both homes and industry if better ways of harnessing the Sun's energy are developed.

TYPES OF SOLAR DEVICES

The most common type of device used to convert solar energy into electricity is called a **photovoltaic cell**. Such cells are made of material that can easily conduct heat and electricity. That material is usually silicon. Sunlight causes electrical charges to flow through the silicon. This is how power is provided to many handheld calculators and wristwatches, as well as to spacecraft and satellites.

Solar conversion systems are another type of solar energy technology. These systems have rows of reflectors that focus sunlight onto fluid-filled pipes or plates. The fluid in the pipes or plates may reach temperatures greater than 750°F (400°C). This heat can be used to warm buildings and to make steam for generating electricity.

Solar collector panels on the roof of a house absorb heat from sunlight. The heat warms liquid flowing in channels inside the collectors. This liquid then flows to a device in the home's basement called a heat exchanger, where water is warmed for household use.

RECENT DEVELOPMENTS A Better Solar Cell

Photovoltaic cells have been made from silicon for more than 50 years. But silicon is expensive—one reason that solar energy systems are so expensive. Many companies are investigating other ways of making solar cells, including using **nanotechnology**. Nanotechnology involves using individual atoms to create larger structures. This technology might lead to new kinds of materials that could be used to make photovoltaic cells.

Shedding Light on Deep Secrets

When we look up at the clear night sky, we can see the vastness of the universe in the infinite points of light. Each of these points is a star, like our Sun. With the aid of a small telescope, we can also see **interstellar** clouds of gas and dust, galaxies other than our own Milky Way, and many other kinds of cosmic objects.

We see these objects because they give off visible light. But did you know that objects that give off visible light make up only a tiny fraction of the universe? Astronomers use telescopes to study the universe in visible light, and they can also use them to study objects in the other ranges of the electromagnetic spectrum. Studies of the most distant visible and invisible light are giving scientists clues to the makeup of the universe, as well as a better understanding of its origin and fate.

OUR EXPANDING UNIVERSE

In the 1920s, American astronomer Edwin Hubble (1889–1953), for whom the Hubble Space Telescope is named, discovered that the universe is expanding. He used a spectrometer on a telescope to spread the light from distant galaxies into their spectra, or rainbows of colors.

Dark lines in the spectra indicated that certain chemicals were present in the galaxies. Light from a motionless object will produce a spectrum with dark lines near the middle of the band of colors. If a light source is moving away from an observer, the lines are closer to the red end of the spectrum. This light is said to be "redshifted." If a light source is moving toward an observer, the lines are closer to the blue end, or "blueshifted."

SCIENCE PIONEERS Edwin Hubble: Discovering New Galaxies

Edwin Hubble was a true scientific revolutionary. He not only discovered that the universe is getting larger, he also disproved the idea that all stars and other objects in space are part of our own Milky Way galaxy. While using a telescope to study a faint, hazy patch in the sky known as the Andromeda Nebula in the 1920s, Hubble noticed that the object appeared to be made of its own stars. This led him to conclude that the nebula is actually a distant galaxy separate from the Milky Way. Astronomers now know that there are billions of other galaxies throughout the universe, each one made of billions of stars.

All the galaxies Hubble viewed were redshifted. The more distant galaxies were more redshifted than closer ones. This was the first sign that the universe is expanding.

All objects in the universe—from planets to stars to galaxies—have the force of gravity exerting a pulling effect around them. Scientists had long thought that the pull of gravity from all the objects in the universe was gradually slowing the expansion of the cosmos. This assumption was proven wrong by new discoveries in the 1990s.

The light from distant objects in space can be spread into colorful spectra that tell astronomers which way the objects are moving. Light from distant galaxies is always "redshifted" because the galaxies are moving away from us. This is evidence that the universe is expanding.

Spectrum of motionless light source

Spectrum of galaxy that is moving away

PICKING UP SPEED

In the late 1990s, two teams of astronomers were studying the light coming from exploding stars called type Ia supernovae. The scientists saw these supernovae as bright spots in galaxies four billion to seven billion light-years away. That means that the stars exploded between four billion and seven billion years ago, but their light is just reaching us now.

The scientists were surprised when they discovered that these supernovae were dimmer than expected. Scientists had thought these stars were at a certain distance and were moving away from Earth at a rather slow speed. The fact that the supernovae were dimmer than expected told the scientists that the stars were farther away and moving away faster than previously believed. This showed that the expansion of the universe is speeding up. Stars and galaxies are speeding away from each other at an increasing rate.

Scientists concluded that this accelerating expansion could happen only if there were some unseen force pushing everything farther and farther apart. Scientists named this force **dark energy**. It has the opposite effect to that of gravity.

Studying the light coming from supernovae in distant galaxies has enabled astronomers to estimate the speed at which the universe is expanding. Some supernovae are brighter than all the other stars in their galaxies. The supernova in this galaxy is visible in the bottom left corner of the photo.

CASE STUDY Seeing Supernovae

Supernovae can be very bright—even outshining the galaxies in which they are located. Chinese astronomers wrote about a supernova in 1054 that was so bright that it could be seen during daytime. This explosion left behind a cloud of gas and dust that can still be seen through telescopes today. This gas cloud is called the Crab Nebula. In 1987, a supernova in a small nearby galaxy called the Large Magellanic Cloud was the first exploding star in almost 400 years that could be seen with the naked eye.

WHAT IS THE UNIVERSE MADE OF?

In 2003, an orbiting telescope named the Wilkinson Microwave Anisotropy Probe (WMAP) took pictures of very distant clumps of light. They are so far away that scientists can tell that the universe was only 380,000 years old when the clumps formed. The type of light captured by WMAP is called cosmic microwave background (CMB) radiation. CMB radiation is not visible light. CMB radiation is like an echo of the Big Bang, the enormous explosion that gave birth to the universe more than 13 billion years ago.

This image, made by the WMAP, shows the most distant—and oldest—light ever seen. The blue spots mark the hottest and highest-energy radiation; the red spots mark the coldest and lowest-energy radiation.

The pulling effects of gravity caused "ripples" in the radiation in the WMAP images. These ripples represented clumps of matter brought together by gravity. Studying the ripples provided scientists with information about how much gravity, matter, and energy are in the universe. By comparing the WMAP images with those made by other telescopes, scientists were able to estimate the amounts of the matter and energy that make up the universe.

HOW DID THE UNIVERSE BEGIN?

By analyzing the WMAP images, scientists reached a number of conclusions about the beginning of the universe. They believe that the Big Bang happened 13.7 billion years ago. Then, in the first fraction of a second of its existence, the super-hot, super-dense universe ballooned in size at an incredibly rapid rate. Finally, although still accelerating, the growth rate slowed to the rate astronomers see today.

LIGHT IS RARE

Astronomers believe that the first stars began to shine about 400 million years after the Big Bang. That is when nuclear fusion reactions started inside the stars. The most distant visible light detected so far dates from when the universe was about 700 million years old.

However, the visible light of all the stars in the sky makes up only a fraction of the universe. According to the most recent estimates based on images from the WMAP and other telescopes, most of the universe—74 percent—is made up of the invisible, mysterious dark energy.

This photo, called the Hubble Ultra Deep Field, shows the most distant—and oldest— visible light ever seen. The Hubble image shows about 10,000 galaxies. The light from these galaxies began traveling to Earth about 13 billion years ago—when the universe was only 700 million years old.

DARK MATTER

Twenty-two percent of the universe consists of exotic, invisible matter known as **dark matter**. Dark matter is different from dark energy. Dark energy is an invisible force that works against gravity; dark matter is invisible material that causes gravity.

Dark matter does not emit, reflect, or absorb electromagnetic radiation. Scientists do not know exactly what it is—but they know it exists because they see how its gravity pulls at galaxies. Galaxies are found in large groups. The gravity holding the galaxies in a group cannot be accounted for with only the visible matter seen in those groups. Therefore, astronomers believe that there must be invisible matter causing this gravitational force.

Dark Energy 74%

Dark Matter 22%

Visible Ordinary Matter 0.5%

Invisible Ordinary Matter 3.5%

Less than one percent of the universe is made up of matter that we can see.

Although scientists are not sure of what dark matter is, they do have some ideas, including **WIMPs** (weakly interacting massive particles). WIMPs are thought to be tiny, but incredibly heavy, particles. These particles are thought to have hundreds of times more mass than protons do.

ORDINARY BUT INVISIBLE

Only the remaining 4 percent of the universe is made of ordinary matter—things such as atoms of hydrogen, oxygen, carbon, and the other chemical elements. However, seven-eighths of this ordinary matter is also invisible. Much of it is in the form of objects that emit types of electromagnetic radiation other than visible light. Such objects include black holes and neutron stars, which are spinning cores of exploded stars.

Thus, only about 0.5 percent of the universe is ordinary matter than can be seen in visible light. This tiny amount of matter accounts for all the stars you see in the sky and all the objects you see on Earth.

WHAT WILL BE THE FATE OF THE UNIVERSE?

Until the discovery in the 1990s that the expansion rate of the universe is increasing, many scientists had thought that the pulling effect of gravity was slowing down the expansion rate. Some scientists thought that this slowdown would eventually cause the universe to become smaller over time. Perhaps a "Big Crunch," in which the universe collapses in on itself, might take place in many billions of years!

But this new information raised questions about what will eventually happen to the universe. Scientist believe that the fate of the universe will probably depend on which force is ultimately proven stronger—gravity pulling things together or dark energy pushing things apart.

RECENT DEVELOPMENTS Destiny Telescope

Destiny—the Dark Energy Space Telescope—is an orbiting observatory that is set to be launched in 2013 to study dark energy. Destiny will observe the distant light from more than 3,000 supernovae as a way of determining how the expansion rate of the universe has changed over billions of years. This will help scientists understand the nature of dark energy and, thus, the fate of the universe.

GRAVITY VS. DARK ENERGY

If dark energy gets weaker over time, the force of gravity might eventually overpower it. Then, the universe might indeed begin to shrink. Perhaps in 100 billion years, everything will be drawn together in a Big Crunch. Some scientists think that a Big Crunch would be followed by a new Big Bang.

But dark energy appears to be stronger than gravity. If it continues to stay stronger, the universe will keep expanding forever. Everything will move farther and farther apart for all time. Perhaps in about 50 billion years, every galaxy, star, and planet—and even every atom—will be torn apart in a "Big Rip."

To determine which of these possible fates awaits the universe—or if there might be some other, unknown fate—scientists are continuing to study the distant and early light of the universe.

SCIENCE PIONEERS Maria Spiropulu: Looking For New Dimensions

Physicists are trying to find WIMPs and other theoretical particles that might provide clues about dark matter, dark energy, and other bizarre phenomena. They are looking for these particles with particle accelerators, large machines that force subatomic (smaller than atoms) particles to collide at high speeds. These collisions create new particles that can then be studied. Maria Spiropulu (born 1970), who works at the CERN facility near Geneva, Switzerland, is using particle accelerators to search for evidence of dimensions beyond the four common dimensions of length, width, depth, and time. According to some theories, there may be as many as six other mysterious dimensions hidden throughout space.

This telescope in New Mexico is part of a project called the Sloan Digital Sky Survey, in which astronomers are making a detailed map of the sky. Researchers use images of distant points of light made with this telescope to discover the locations and distances of many millions of galaxies.

Lighting the Way

Visible light makes up only a tiny fraction of the universe. Yet it is enormously important. It makes all the stars shine, including our own Sun. Without the light of the Sun, there could be no life on Earth. Plants, animals, and virtually all other organisms depend on light for survival.

For thousands of years, the only light sources people had were the natural sources of the Sun and fire. Then, such simple inventions as candles, torches, and oil lamps enabled people to use light for warmth and to see in the dark. With later inventions, including eyeglasses, microscopes, and cameras, people used the properties of light, such as reflection and refraction, to improve their lives and further their understanding of the world.

The invention of the electric light ushered in new eras in industry, science, and everyday life. Lasers and fiber optics gave people new ways to benefit from light. We owe our communications systems, surgical procedures, CDs, DVDs, and many other technologies to light.

CASE STUDY Super Bowl Holograms

At the Super Bowl in Detroit, Michigan, in February 2006, security guards watched 3-D holograms of people in the stands to help them better identify known terrorists. The holography system, developed by Intrepid Defense & Security Systems of Birmingham, Michigan, consisted of two cameras that acted as right and left eyes to project 3-D images onto a screen. Special picture tubes in the monitors made the images appear as if they were rising 30 inches (76 centimeters) from, and sinking 30 inches into, the screen.

Solar energy systems use sunlight to provide people with electric power and warmth. Some day, we may use the energy of light for much of our electric power. Who knows what other future technological developments will be based on light?

KNOWLEDGE AND POWER

The universe is filled with light—some of it visible, most of it invisible. Studies of the most distant light in the universe are providing new insights into scientists' deepest questions concerning the composition, origin, and ultimate fate of the universe.

So you might say that light gives us a source of life, power, and understanding. Think of that the next time you click on a light switch in your home!

Light holds the key to discovering the answer to what is perhaps the most profound question we can ask: What is the ultimate fate of the universe? The continuing study of photons streaming from such distant galaxies as this one, which is about 60 million light-years away, may eventually enable us to answer this question.

Further Resources

MORE BOOKS TO READ

Bova, Ben. *The Story of Light.* Naperville, Ill.: Sourcebooks, 2001.

Cobb, Vicki. *Open Your Eyes: Discover Your Sense of Sight.* Brookfield, Conn.: Millbrook Press, 2002.

Farndon, John. *From Newton's Rainbow to Frozen Light: Discovering Light.* Chicago: Heinemann Library, 2007.

Silverstein, Alvin, Virginia Silverstein, and Laura Silverstein Nunn. *Seeing.* Breckenridge, Colo.: 21st Century Books, 2001.

Stille, Darlene R. *Manipulating Light: Reflection, Refraction, and Absorption.* Minneapolis: Compass Point, 2006.

USING THE INTERNET

Explore the Internet to find out more about light. You can use a search engine such as kids.yahoo.com and type in keywords such as **light**, **visible spectrum**, **electromagnetic spectrum**, and **laser**.

These search tips will help you find useful websites more quickly:

• Know exactly what you want to find out about first.

• Use only a few important keywords in a search, putting the most relevant words first.

• Be precise. Only use names of people, places, or things.

Glossary

albedo effect effect on a region's climate of an object's brightness and the amount of light it reflects or absorbs

amplitude distance from a peak (high point) or trough (low point) to the midpoint of a wave

angle of incidence angle at which light strikes a surface

angle of reflection angle at which light rebounds from a surface

atom smallest complete unit of matter

aurora streamers or bands of light that appear in the sky at night, especially in polar regions

bioluminescence production of visible light by certain animals and organisms

black hole region of space with such a strong gravitational force that nothing—not even light—can escape

circadian rhythm daily cycle of changes in a person's alertness, body temperature, and organ function

coherent light light in which the wave peaks and troughs move together

concave curved inward like the inside of a bowl

convex curved outward at the center

dark energy mysterious force that is causing the expansion of the universe to accelerate

dark matter invisible material that does not emit, reflect, or absorb any kind of electromagnetic radiation

diabetic retinopathy condition in which blood vessels in the retina leak, close up, or grow too much, causing blood to fill the inside of the eyeball

diffraction spreading out of light waves as they pass through small openings or near the edges of small objects

dispersion spreading of white light into its various colors

electrode conductor through which an electric current is passed

electromagnetic radiation energy that flows through space as both waves and particles

electromagnetic spectrum band of electromagnetic radiation arranged in order of wavelength

electron negatively charged particle in an atom

endoscope fiber-optic device that is passed through a small incision, enabling a doctor to view the inside of a patient's body

fiber optics branch of physics concerned with the transmission of light through transparent "optical" fibers of glass or plastic

fluorescence type of luminescence in which a substance emits light only as long as it is exposed to the source of exciting energy

frequency number of waves that pass a particular point per second

gravity force of attraction between all objects

holography method for storing and displaying a three-dimensional image, usually on a photographic plate called a hologram

hyperopia farsightedness; condition in which a person has trouble seeing nearby objects clearly

incandescence type of light production in which heat is emitted with light

incoherent light light that consists of waves of many different wavelengths (colors); ordinary light is incoherent

interstellar refers to the space between stars

irradiation use of gamma rays to destroy bacteria in food and on surgical instruments

light-year distance that light travels in a year—5.88 trillion miles (9.46 trillion kilometers)

luminescence giving off of light without emitting much, if any, heat

luminous intensity amount of light produced by a source

macula cone-rich area in the retina that provides the sharpest vision

mass amount of matter in an object

molecule combination of two or more atoms; for example, a molecule of water consists of two atoms of hydrogen and one atom of oxygen

myopia nearsightedness; condition in which a person has trouble seeing distant objects clearly

nanotechnology using individual atoms to create larger structures

nebula cloud of gas and dust in space

nuclear fusion combination of two atomic nuclei to create a nucleus of greater mass, giving off energy

opaque material that does not let light through; not transparent

optical illusion visual image that is deceptive or misleading

orbit travel around a larger object in a curving path

oscillation back-and-forth movement

phosphor chemical substance inside the tubes of fluorescent lights that gives off visible light but very little heat

photosynthesis use of sunlight, water, and carbon dioxide by plants to make carbohydrates and oxygen

photovoltaic cell A device that changes sunlight directly into electricity

prism glass or quartz object that refracts white light into all of its colors

quartz a colorless, transparent mineral

retina thin layer of specialized cells at the inside back of the eyeball that absorbs light and converts it into electrical signals

scattering spreading of light rays in all directions when they strike tiny particles, such as molecules in the air

solar wind stream of energetic particles that flows from the Sun

spectrometer device that spreads out a substance's light into colors that correspond to the chemical makeup of the substance

stimulated emission process in which a photon stimulates an atom to emit another photon; the second photon is of equal energy to, and moving in the same direction as, the first photon

supernova exploding star

translucent material that lets some light through but is not able to be seen through clearly

transparent material through which light can easily pass

vacuum empty space without even air in it

visible spectrum wavelengths of the electromagnetic spectrum that can be seen by the human eye

wavelength distance from the peak (high spot) or trough (low point) of one wave to the same point on the next wave

WIMP weakly interacting massive particle; a theoretical particle that is very tiny but incredibly heavy

Index